What Does a Scientist Use?

E. Cardenas
N. Delgado

MILO EDUCATIONAL BOOKS & RESOURCES

www.miloeducationalbooks.com

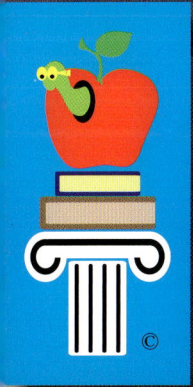

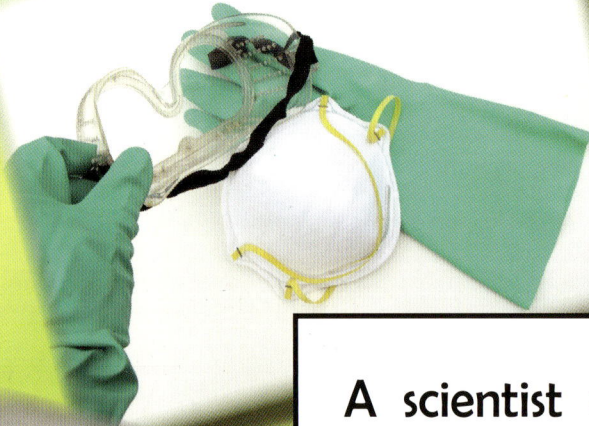

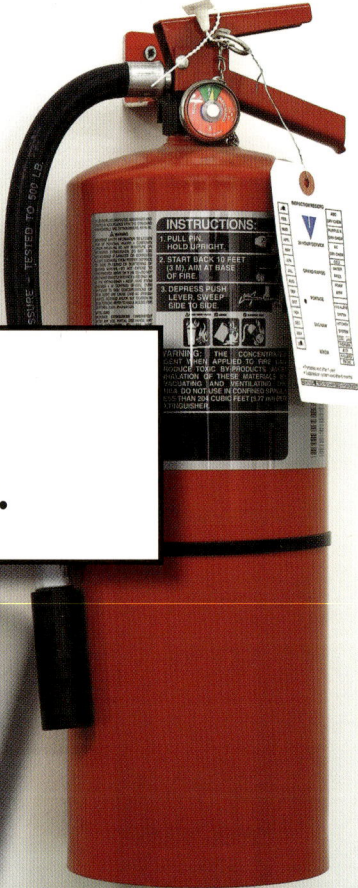

A scientist uses
safety equipment.

2

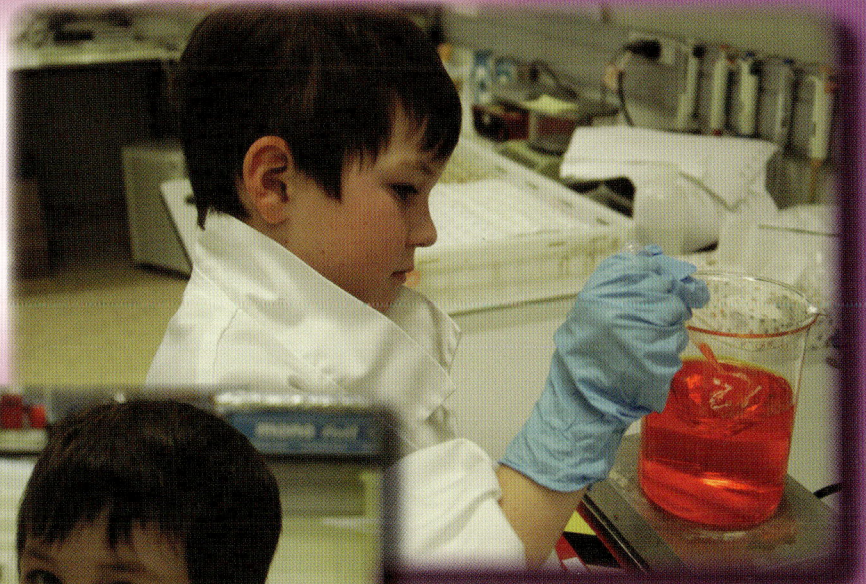

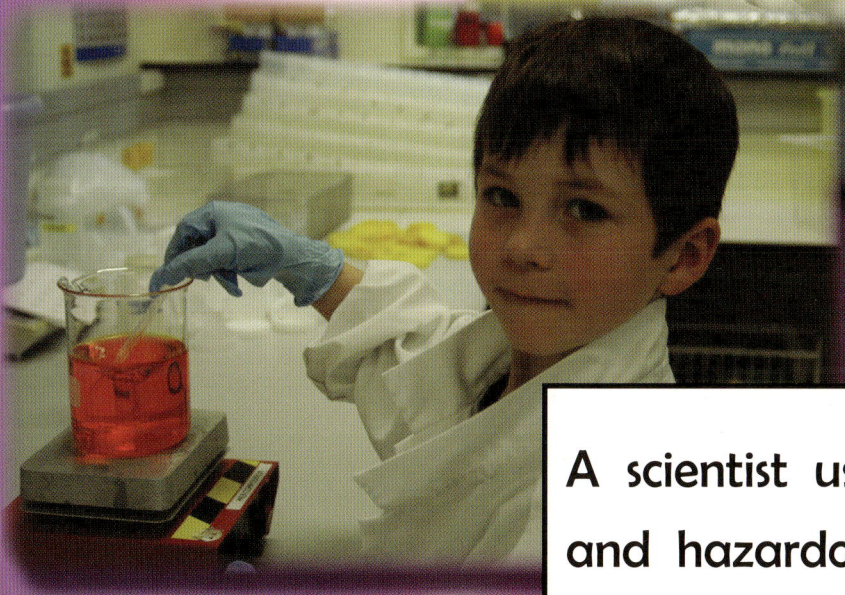

A scientist uses fragile objects
and hazardous materials.

3

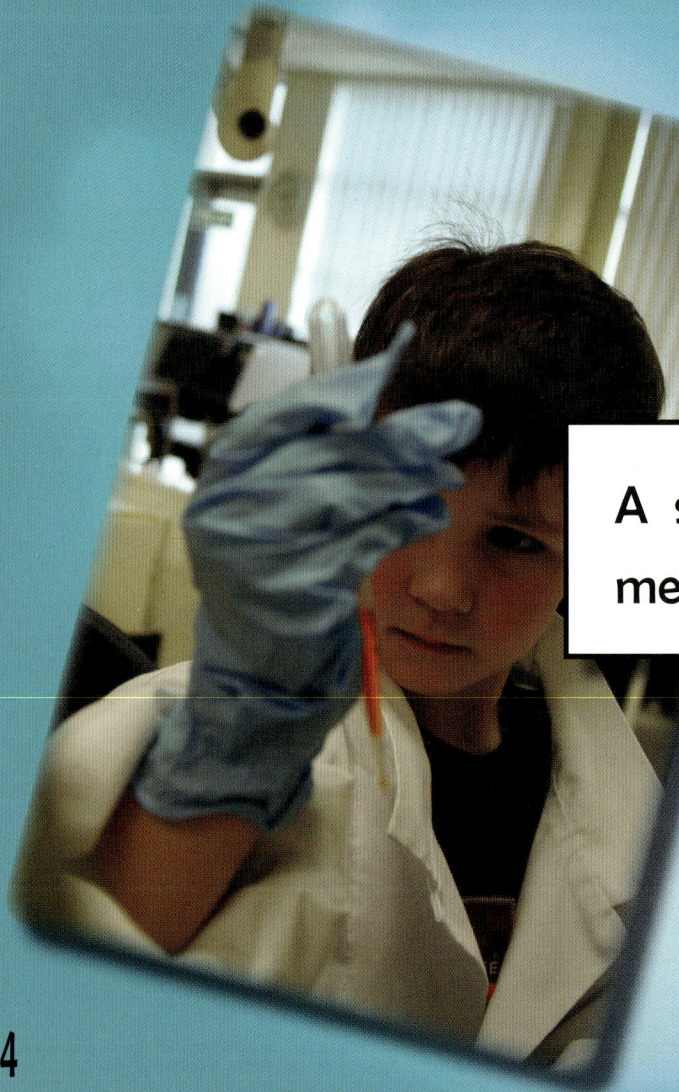

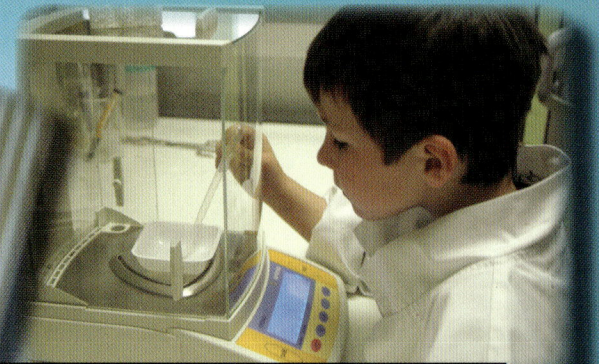

A scientist uses different measuring instruments.

A scientist uses scales, thermometers, timers, and rulers to measure.

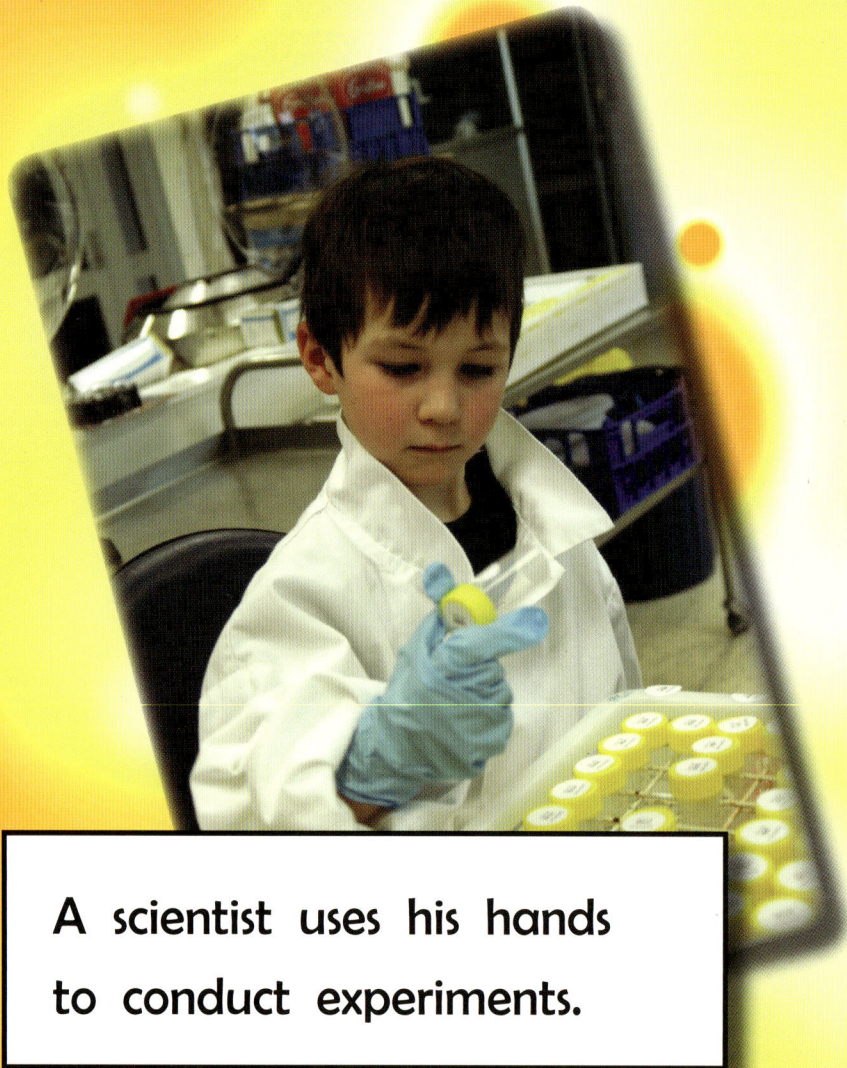

A scientist uses his hands
to conduct experiments.

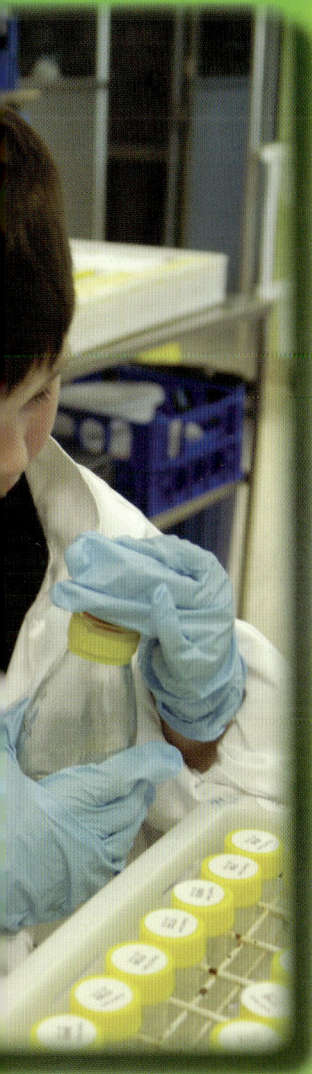

But what a scientist uses the most is...

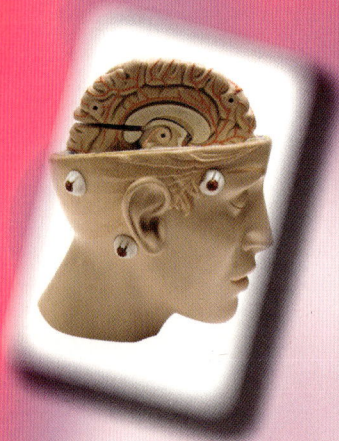

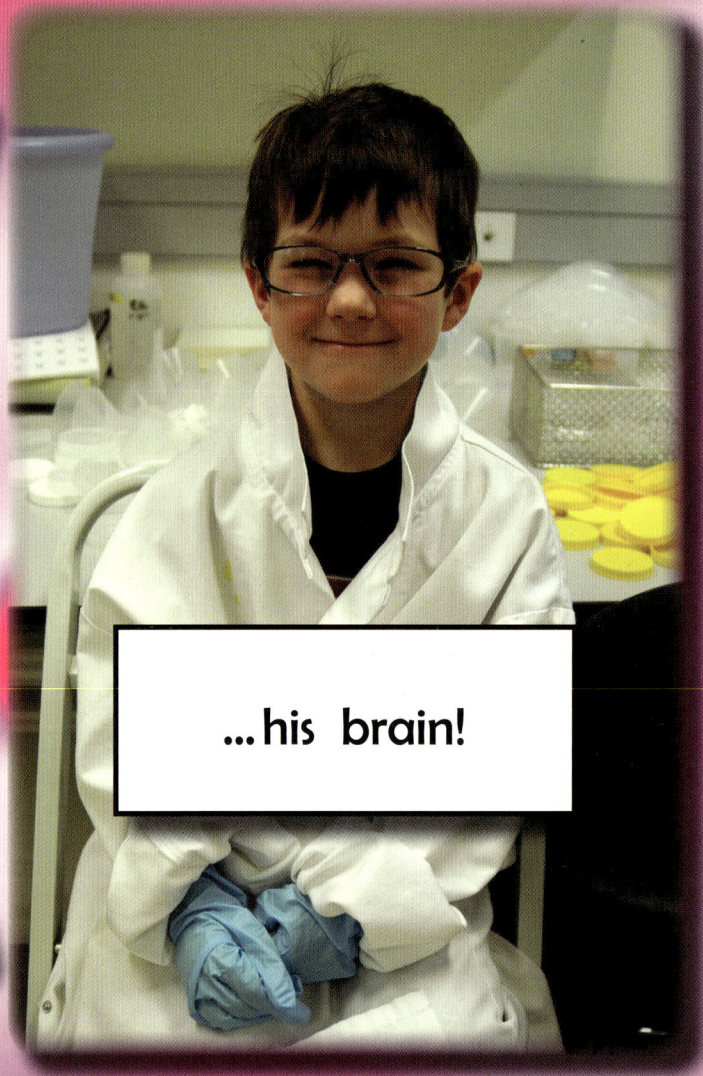

...his brain!

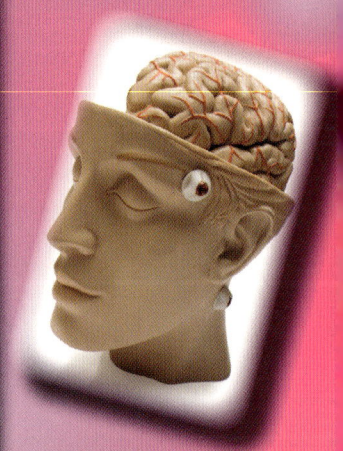